ONE HOUSE | TWO MINDS

The Psychological Effects of COVID-19 on Our Household

Written By:

The Durrs

Intro

Therapy is just a search for the source code to your problems. What better metric to use other than honesty when embarking on that psychological voyage? This book started out as written notes to each other in an attempt to salvage our union during these perilous times of the COVID-19 pandemic. After reading each other's notes and simultaneously watching news clips of peaking domestic violence around the country due to the effects of this pandemic, we later felt like our writings may have some empirical connections to others that may be going through similar psychological turmoil as we have faced. Therefore, we collaged our notes into a book with the hopes that people may read and relate.

In the last chapter, "Collaborative Solutions," we set out to do something never done before! Instead of writing down our solutions, we inserted a QR-code so that readers can use their smart phones to scan the code and be taken directly to a video which shows us discussing our problems and figuring out solutions.

We hope our examples of collecting our thoughts together and thoughtfully talking through them as a union will inspire others to continue to work through this unexpected, tough time and prevail forward.

The Newborn
from the perspective of Sarah Durr

If someone would have predicted Darwin and I would have already had our first child together by our 1st wedding anniversary, I would have believed them. You're probably thinking, "Um, but don't people usually say they *wouldn't* have believed it?" Yeah, they do. But I said what I said. It wasn't a secret how enthusiastic I was to start – or, as I usually refer to our dynamic – to continue our family.

When Darwin and I first started dating, I wasted no time in making it clear to him how important family was to me. I'm just one branch stemming from a large family tree, myself, and although "the more, the crazier" seems to be the trend in my family… I still wouldn't trade any of them for any other. In my culture, it's just about a rite of passage to bear children. A few, at minimum. These days, of course, things have transitioned greatly from my grandmother's story: She married at 12 years old, had her first child by 14, and continued having children until age 46. If you're following along with the math here, she made it to a total of 17 pregnancies, with 13 born children who all lived to at least middle age. And, that's just on my mom's side! Add my dad's side of the family and in total I have 12 uncles, 10 aunts, and a number of first cousins that I stopped counting a long time ago. (Yes, that number is <u>still</u> growing.)

Some people who come from big families grow older seeking isolation and silence, becoming somewhat of a recluse, even. This was not the case for me. I kind of love the "crazy" that comes along with the many personalities I have to deal with. To me, the most beautiful aspect that makes families just that is the fact that we don't get to choose them. Almost like those co-workers we don't particularly like. Naturally, we gravitate towards others with like-minds or similar interests… but then there's that bunch of select co-workers you look at with the side eye and just wonder who birthed them. Your mind originally tells you there's no way you'd ever spend time with these people outside the confines of your workplace, but little by little, they start to grow on you. Even that one you just envisioned and made a face about.

It's those kinds of differences between us that make our relationships especially extraordinary. We learn a lot from these people; what we do like, what we don't. A difference in perspective is not only food for thought, but also it's necessary for us to discover *why* we believe in what we do. And more often than not, that is something we just won't typically get from our hand-picked, like-minded buddies. But with our family — we simply don't get the choice. It's a necessary confliction. All that to say: Our family becomes our first teachers of life. And whether you grow to love or hate the instructors surrounding… you still come out with lessons that shape you into the individual who you become.

In my family, things are far from perfect. We fight, we argue, we stop talking for long periods; but, we always find ourselves back at some point. And that's the part I cherish so much. Now that I have my own family, old ideas of what a family is are being reshaped. Don't get me wrong, the trend is still "the more, the crazier" on both sides. But now, we're creating our own, new memories in new roles.

Within this short period of time, families have gone through so much together. Mine included. For starters, our daughter was born at the height of it all. We got lucky with the timing considering that had she been born just a couple of weeks later, there would have been a pretty good chance that I would have had to deliver her at the hospital alone. Due to COVID-19, some hospitals restricted birth deliveries to only the mother, not allowing any partners to be present because of social distancing. Not trying to sound like an alarmist—but could you imagine that?! A first-time mom, going through labor and delivery (as if that isn't nerve-wrecking enough), without any emotional support, in a hospital or health-care facility that could possibly be housing patients who are sick with a non-preventable, non-treatable illness!? And forget what that may mean about my health as the mother… WHAT ABOUT THE HEALTH OF MY BABY??? We definitely lucked up with that timing. The stress of falling ill with the unknown coronavirus would be enough stress in its own right, but you throw a newborn baby into the mix and that's a whole other level of stress.

Luckily, we had a safe delivery with a beautiful, healthy baby girl we call Zehn… but the stress doesn't end there. For the first three weeks of our daughter's life, we were serenaded by tons of extended family (of course) and slowly, we all watched the news go from telling us what's going on globally to feeling the effects in our own lives. I can recall it all so vividly. First, it was my husband's job. Amid us getting used to having a newborn in our household, Darwin was laid off with not a single clue as to when things would pick back up. This was just the beginning of the mass confusion that we had no idea was soon to come.

As the entire nation shut down, one state after the next, the future was becoming very blurry in our household. Our household now had no steady income with four mouths to feed. Every day of 24/7 news coverage was like watching the hands of the clock circulate. Tick, tick, tick. We watched as the country reacted in so many ways. On the one hand, we had the group of innovators who created brand-new organizations mainly in efforts to help others in need during the crisis. (My husband was in this group.) Then, we had the panickers who were cleaning out all the grocery stores when they heard businesses were closing. They must not have seen the part about essential services (i.e. grocery stores) staying open. For God's sake, people were buying up all the toilet papers as if this virus was said to have caused diarrhea as a symptom. (I'll never understand it.) And then lastly, there was the social media group. These people pretty much spent all of their time swiping through TikTok videos attempting to go viral for their 15 minutes of fame. But each of these groups of people all had one thing in common: Wondering when the hell the country was going to go back to normal.

So, let's add up all the levels of stress thus far. There's a global pandemic spreading like wildfire, we run the risk of becoming ill if we go outside, we have a newborn with a still-developing immune system who could also fall sick, our only current source of income is depleted for the time being, and we have no idea as to when it will restore. I lost count at "newborn." Oh, and did I mention that some weeks into the shutdown our daughter got sick? Don't worry — it wasn't the coronavirus that she had, but many of her symptoms were that of the virus alike, so it gave us grave cause for concern without a doubt. The paranoia was haunting me. My first experience looking after a newborn and I have to constantly decipher what is and isn't normal during a time where the risk of bringing her into a hospital, or even her pediatrician's office, may result in something much, much worse.

Every day of this thing is a limbo. I think the whole country wakes up and goes to bed every night wondering the same thing: "How much longer?! And, where do we go from here??" Not just that, but Darwin wakes up with what seems to be a different idea almost every day. And that can be translated in a lot of different ways, but one way I saw it meant: "If ever I planned to _____, (fill in the blank), like let's say… hmm, I don't know… maybe try to take a shower at some point today, I'd have to find a way to make sure I could be relieved from our daughter." It might not seem like it should be too challenging to accomplish, but believe me, it becomes quite the task when he's running around constantly looking for something [else] to do and I'm home tip-toeing around the sleeping baby. Then, when I do get some kind of chance to eat, use the bathroom, etc., it's like the anxiety spewing from Darwin's ears are hard not to notice. It becomes so frustrating because I hate to be rushed, especially when he's vividly showing me that whatever "favor" he thinks he's doing me is being done begrudgingly. At that point, I'm thinking, "Just give me the damn baby, then!"

You know how people make the comment, "Yeah, having a baby is a full-time job!" Sure, they mean well, but honestly, having a full-time job is not even comparable to being the primary caregiver of a newborn. That would be an understatement. At least full-time jobs allow for workers to go home and get relieved from one shift until the next. There are labor laws, for goodness sake. But being a full-time parent means the only "breaks" you may get are the slim chances you have to actually get other responsibilities done (e.g. cook, clean, wash clothes, etc.). And don't even think about vacuuming while the baby is asleep! Anything to keep the baby asleep!

I also hope this isn't coming off to some of you as me complaining about being a responsible parent—I'd just like to get a chance to take a shower a few times a week and use the toilet as my body requests. And if I were taking care of her as a single parent that would also be different, but I'm not. I'm in a marriage where my husband and I are both unemployed during this pandemic, home with a newborn. I just wish I could get in the shower, or have a brief moment to myself, without having to go through the ringer to make arrangements for my baby girl. Is that really asking for a lot?

Being a newlywed couple is already a new chapter to explore, but learning to co-parent with your spouse is another. With my step-son, I've always maintained boundaries to the extent of my parenting him. While I may have discussed important decisions concerning my step-son with my husband throughout the duration of our relationship, I always treaded carefully with my input because even prior to having our daughter, I always understood that no one likes to be criticized for their parenting. But things are different now considering I am now the other co-parent.

Most couples take on different roles of parenting. It's funny how life works. I always gave my own mother a hard time for always being "the bad guy" (her words) between her and my father's parenting styles, and here it is now looking like I'll have to bear the burden of that same perception for the lack of enforcement coming from Zehn's father. I mean, I understand that it's still extremely early in our parenting journey together – and the current circumstances are also temporarily affecting our lives and psyches – but I feel like this is setting a foundation of what we become comfortable with. If you ask him, his [somewhat] distance is due to sacrificing time right now for future fiscal gain, and I believe that, but I do worry he will get too comfortable with this dynamic. Right now, Zehn knows Daddy is the guy who makes her laugh when he's home. It's the "when he's home" part that troubles me. I know this period of time will pass and I have faith that we will power through it, but the contemplation of not being able to foresee the lasting effects that come from this pandemic on my household's structure has played a big part on my psyche.

The Newborn
from the perspective of Darwin Durr

I watch Zehn's two-month-old eyes attentively follow something invisible that I cannot see. She laughs at this physics-defying thing as it flies all around the room, according to her wandering eyes. I feel like sunlight creeps through the blinds sometimes just to say hello to her. She giggles and responds with a drooling droplet rolling down her puffy cheek. With no comprehension of a pillow, she uses the comfort of my chest to lay her head and dream her first dreams. She cries, not always of pain, but as an alerting language in need of parental deciphering by her mom and I. She causes me to shun the notion that we are all born sinners, for she's dressed fully in a divine coating. She has reformed my belief, leading me to believe that we are all born comprised of innocence and that the devil meets us down the road. How dare the COVID-19 interrupt these moments?

A promising tomorrow looks vague each day that COVID-19 paralyzes our minds, health, and livelihood. My household is hemorrhaging stabilizing resources right now due to me being laid off because of this pandemic. The foundation of my home is beginning to replicate crumbling pillars. All of this is happening during the same time that our home has been graced with a beautiful newborn baby girl. The psychological ramifications of these intersecting events create a hyper-tension mindset that tends to blockade everything else from entering my mind. I begin to direct all of my thoughts towards survival. So, the mental wrestling match becomes, "How do I create a diverged mindset where one is tailored to survival, and one is tailored to the enjoyment of my newborn?" The answer is, "I don't know."

As a wolf, I feel like moments like now require a sacrificial stance. The question becomes, "Do I use my newborn daughter's youthful unawareness to my advantage, and become somewhat evasive due to fully targeting a solution for our household with the hopes that I succeed before her awareness begins to materialize? Or, do I let emotions distract me from the larger picture, which is doing anything and everything possible to ensure that my household is stable?"

This binary war in my head disturbs my wife. I don't think she understands the wolf mentality. I believe we view the love for our newborn daughter in different contexts. She sees the nurture, while I see survival. When it comes to nurture and comfort, it's hard for me to falsely smile in glee when pandemonium is searing through my thoughts.

Encapsulated within this psychological rut, I find no space or time for the futile components of the world. Leisure has met its demise. I'm quickly flustered by anything that doesn't fit within the fulfillment of my three-prong ravenous cravings: food, shelter, and finances. COVID-19 has turned all of my therapeutic hobbies into fulltime attempts to materialize a dream. When they were just hobbies, the failing of them were laughable. Now, they're self-inflicted wounds every time they lift from the ground and fail to defy gravity. I feel like this is making me a bad father. I'm caught within a gravitational pull away from my daughter's most precious moments because while racing the clock of a severe disaster, I find almost no time on the clock to enjoy her smile.

Even when my ideas find a paralyzed state and I'm just sitting there staring, I can vividly see that my wife could use a temporary relief from Zehn – but it's this fear of "if I relieve Sarah, I run the risk of missing that highly anticipated thought that will ignite my next project." A project that will potentially help us pay our rent and sustain our livelihood. The moment I pick up Zehn, I will be stolen and thrust into her messianic presence for a time that can't be recollected. While many may say "what's wrong with that?" I would say that it's the pressures of the clock. Knowing that catastrophe is approaching, psychologically it's hard for me to not use all of my seconds trying to halt its arrival.

If my mind is not occupied within productivity during the day, my anxiety reaches suicide levels due to a feeling of worthlessness. Since COVID-19 has forced me out of a job, in the last sixty days I've hand-stitched and sold over one-hundred masks, written two books and self-published them to Amazon – this book being the second and my first being a fictional novel named, *Satan's Old Piano,* and lastly my biggest project yet during this juncture, a brand new mobile video game available worldwide on iOS and Android named, *Mr. President, I Found The Cure - A DURR GAME.* Even with being blessed to have the competence to complete three massive projects within sixty days, I'm still sitting here wide-eyed and anxiety is climbing a high precipice because none of these projects have had enough time to flourish, but the clock doesn't care! It just keeps ticking and bills are due now!

Early on in this mind-fracturing time of COVID-19, I actually considered going dark and entering the sphere of criminality. Downloading *Tor* and surfing the Dark Web for jobs that would pay up to $10,000. That's how steep my depression became – because when a man is stripped of his ability to keep his family stable, his moral compass begins to spin in a frenzy. I was willing to sacrifice everything just to keep comfort being the aura of my household. However, I analyzed that risk and it was too outlandish to pursue. I quickly remembered that I am a man of high productivity and that if I fail, I should fail trying my hardest in a dignified manner. Zehn needs her dad around.

Tension between my wife and I are starting to bloom over Zehn. My wife and I differ slightly on the reported accuracy of the COVID-19. I feel like it has a minute tilt to being an alarmist, fear-mongering narrative. *I AM NEITHER DOWNPLAYING THE VIRUS NOR DISRESPECTING ANYONE WHO HAS DIED FROM THE VIRUS* I'm only speaking to the stress and confrontational energy that has been brewing in my household in reference to Zehn's health. The information that we see daily on the news is so conflicting that it causes cognitive chaos in my brain. First, Americans were told to not wear a mask. Then, later, we were told to wear them, and some states mandated their use. Then, Americans were told that kids weren't really at risk and that it was primarily the elderly or people with already pre-existing medical conditions. Now, three months later and over one-million cases reported in the US thus far — NOW, there are new reports that it is starting to affect kids with a Kawasaki-like illness. Hummm… Three months later and over one-million cases already reported and now… Kids?

Under normal circumstances, when your child sneezes, coughs, or has diarrhea, you know all the things newborns naturally display already, you don't find your sanity teetering a thin line – but because of COVID-19 there's no worst thought than your precious newborn potentially having a virus that is being reported as being deadly. This is another contributing distortion to the enjoyment of Zehn's beginnings. Every sneeze, we're debating over the severity of it. The symptoms of COVID-19 are so broad that they're synonymous with everyday common cold occurrences. Can you imagine the psychological burden of thinking everything means potential death? It makes you question God. If God were to snatch Zehn from us via a virus, how does one ever look at the sky again?

When I look at the tampering of our civil liberties during COVID-19, it makes me wonder what kind of future my daughter will endure. I see stories of police drones hovering in the air, in an attempt to control a citizenry. I went to the grocery store the other day and the Army National Guard was guarding the entryway. I see stories of police officers physically assaulting and arresting non-violent Americans because they're not wearing masks. I saw a story of a Texas woman jailed for trying to feed her children by opening her hair salon a few days before Mother's Day. I watched the government treat its citizens like we were incompetent by telling us that "we" didn't need masks, but the hospitals did. Just to address the American people weeks later with a contradictory statement urging everyone now to wear masks or some sort of face covering. I fear that my daughter may not get a chance to know the world that I once knew three months ago. A world where America was free.

Being a man tailored more to the archaic principles of being a man, ideologically, I feel like I should be the nucleus and foundational structure of my home. That's not to sound patriarchal or to take away from my wife because unlike me, she has a bachelor's degree and is very capable of being the head of household. But I would be lying if I said that this juncture is not a psychological struggle within my head knowing that I'm a wolf unable to hunt. I just pray that at least one of these three seeds (two books and a mobile video game) that I planted within the last sixty days begins to show some promise – because employment doesn't. My daughter's smile is waiting for me, but I have to make sure that she eats.

Having a newborn has presented itself to be hard, especially being born in conjunction with a global pandemic. I never imagined myself having another child, but once I married Sarah, I felt like I had an obligation to not deprive her of the parental experience of having a child of her own. I already have a 13-year-old son named, Jaccai. He also lives with us. He's just entering that mind space of "somewhat" independent. A stage that most parents yearn for. You know… that moment when your child moves off to college and you discreetly cheer because of the solace that re-enters your home lol.

Secretly wishing that your child hurries up and grows out of your hair doesn't mean that you don't love them. If you're a parent, then you know exactly what I mean. So, here it is that Jaccai is so close to that "do it yourself" age, and here comes the beautiful, messianic Zehn! "Make room for me, Daddy" – her smile shouts! I love my newborn with all my heart, but this borderline catastrophe that my household is facing distracts me so much.

I'm developing a monstrous fatigue of the mounting problems that're beginning to wear me down. Three months of dormancy feels like three years. If honesty were to seep through my worn-out courageous mask, it would show that I'm ready to give up. It feels like I'm struggling to hold the world up and someone has just added the moon atop. What happens if my buckling knees cause my shoulders to drop both? What troubles me the most is that I honestly don't know if my wife would be prepared to take the helm. It's almost as if she doesn't see that there are a multitude of things to juggle, not just Zehn. And because my wife offers no solutions on our theoretical house blackboard, I'm tasked with doing the juggling. I think she gets so narrow-minded and only sees my minute evasiveness of Zehn, but she doesn't see the reasoning. If I don't hunt, who will? If I don't plan, who will? If I don't push, who will?

Oh, did I mention that I'm now a high-school-degree-having teacher?! COVID-19 has caused every school in Washington, DC to close and lessons have abruptly migrated to the home. Jaccai shows me math equations with 26 alphabets and 26 numbers, seems like, and my head spins like the exorcist! Added pressure! From my observations, what I've noticed is that being home confiscates a certain degree of attention. It's atmospheric psychology. A person tends to do best within an environment solely designed for whatever area of focus that they are tasked to perform. For example, a person tends to be a lot more motivated in the gym versus exercising at home, in my opinion. It's the same for remote learning. The PlayStation controller just sits there and smiles at the child. Calling their name like a friend. The couch and bed yawn in a transference manner, bottling the child in a relaxed aura.

Prior to this massive household change to remote learning, I admit, I wasn't hard temperament-wise towards Jaccai. He's an honor roll student, so that alone caused me to be very easy on him. Now, I'm finding myself having to be oddly stern. This abrupt change is causing a foreign friction between my son and me. Why? Because since he's been remote learning, I trusted that he was correctly doing his work and responsibly participating in his Zoom classes with his teachers. Come to discover, he's operating to the complete contrary. He's completing half of his work and his PlayStation controller is glued to his hand while his teachers are teaching over the computer. "AHHHH!" I scream in my head! More pressure! How am I to sit in the house everyday ensuring that Jaccai is properly executing his school duties while at the same time, chase and hunt opportunities that will bring a dollar into our home? I really feel like I'm being screwed. The apparatus of my household is really coming apart. My wife probably thinks that I don't love my daughter. My son is becoming a major problem. Bills are due. Money is nearly depleted. Food cabinets are rumbling like empty stomachs. Time is not slowing and allowing me to catch up. Oh, and there's a notice in my building that says someone in here died of COVID-19, but for privacy reasons they're not releasing their name. Hold on… WHAT!

The Finances
from the perspective of Sarah Durr

Do I look for a job outside of the home? Do I pick up driving in my spare time? Wait – what spare time?!

If I work from home, will I still need someone to look after our daughter? There's no way I'll be able to focus on her AND working a job at the same time.

Weighing the cons of each option I come up with are deterring. I know this may come off somewhat selfish, but the most important thing to me is knowing how my daughter is being looked after on a daily basis. Before the pandemic even occurred, I decided it would be best to stay home with our daughter after she was born. There wasn't a concrete plan in place for when I would return to work, or where for that matter, but I was utterly in fear of sending her off to a day care as a newborn baby. Multiply that by ten now that we're living through a global pandemic. I say this may come off as selfish not because of my innate protectiveness—I won't apologize for my maternal instinct. The reason is because I realize it puts a lot more pressure on my husband to hold down the entire household financially. And you may be of a more conservative mindset and might be thinking, "Men have been doing that for ages. What's the big deal?" Sure, that's one way of looking at it—but I'm going to be honest and really dive into why it is somewhat selfish of me.

For starters, up until this point I've never had to be "taken care of," so the subject in itself makes me uneasy; the feeling of not being able to fiscally contribute to our household. I don't like feeling like a burden. (I know, I know — "but, it's your husband.") Still. It's foreign for me. Maybe I should put it into perspective for those of you who may not understand that feeling. Imagine a man who is not working, his wife is taking care of everything in the household and his ego is damaged. That's it, that's the perspective. (For some reason, people seem to comprehend that men have egos much more easily than the idea that women have them, too.) So, it's the same thing for me.

To be honest, my husband is the first man I've had a relationship with where the guy wasn't more reliant on me than I was on him. In retrospect, that may have been a quality I was attracted to so that I wouldn't ever have to feel like my independence was compromised. I remember early on in our relationship, we both used to feel so compelled to pay each other back for every, single thing the other person picked up. Something as insignificant as a Starbucks latte was a reason for us to hide money in each other's possession so our egos could be fed. It's entirely laughable now, but that's how serious we were about "having our own."

Now here we are, just past our 1st anniversary of marriage with a newborn and living through a pandemic that has caused tremendous financial hardship for us, much like many other Americans. My husband was laid off from his job, which was taking care of our entire household pre-pandemic, at the start of the shutdown. Every day since then, I've watched as my husband racked his mind trying to come up with a new plan to get us through it all. This man takes no breaks. All day. Every day. I have to say, as I'm writing this— my man is actually so amazing, and too often I allow my emotion-of-the-day to blind me to that. (Note: I mean, I did just have a baby, so these hormones have not given me a break in just about a year now, but I'm just saying!)

You see, one difference between him and I is that many times my mind becomes one-tracked in any given situation, while his seems to always be looking at it from an aerial view. Big picture. This is a trait I truly admire about this guy. I learned before that introverts (such as my husband) are much more calculated in the way they arrive at their thoughts. As you could probably guess from the previous sentence, yes! I do tend to be more of an extrovert. Extroverts are more likely to think quickly in conversational response, which is how we're always entertaining others. On the contrary, introverts tend to take a bit longer to ponder before answering a question because they're carefully mapping out all moves ahead. Much like chess (as he always reminds me). With this in mind, I tend to also live in the moment and he's a bit more like a year or two from now. That kind of ideological difference can (and does) cause many disputes between any couple. But since we've been living through the coronavirus pandemic, these kinds of disputes have become magnified.

With that said, my lack of planning mixed with the unexpected blows from the coronavirus have left us trying to pick up the pieces amid it all. Along with much of the other stress being piled on from daily pandemic updates, I can't help but feel like I've caused a great deal of anguish within this household and in this marriage, frankly. Darwin has this unbelievable foresight of prophesizing the future, but the Aries in me often disregards the 'heads-up' suggestions and carries on with my own way of doing things. I must admit with honestly that my judgment could use a bit of help sometimes. Many times, actually. (It's so much easier to admit this in writing rather than in-person. I told you, I'm an Aries.)

Another aspect to all of this that may have very well discreetly played a role in our recent battles is the fact that my psychology had already been affected pre-COVID-19. As in, I just went through 9 months of pregnancy and then birthed a baby—just in case anyone had forgotten. For nearly one whole year now, my hormones have been taken through a ferris-wheel of surprises, resulting in plenty of cloudy, brain fog and upsets that usually would not have even crossed my mind a second time around. Aside from the emotional fragment, I'm aware that my focus has been greatly redirected to a much narrower scope of my role in our union. I had been awaiting this special moment in my life for my entire life, so becoming Zehn's mom has become my sole focus. And as I mentioned prior, I often become so caught up in one detail sometimes that I don't even see what doesn't fall into the purview of the blinders. So yes, that means other people's needs, too. In this case, including my husband's. (Even my own self-care at times, now that she's arrived.) But with my husband, I know I've let him down a handful of times throughout the past year and that brings me remorse for not consciously playing every role I should have played to keep us strong, not just my wide eyes for having my own first child. So, when I said in the introduction of this chapter that my choices in relation to our daughter's arrival are somewhat selfish, this is what I meant. I'm owning up to my part of pretty much leaving my husband to figure things out for us financially while I lived in the realms of glee for my dream coming into fruition, while he still has dreams of his own.

So now that all of that is off my chest, the question remains: "Where do we go from here?" A great question, indeed. Reaching this point of realization would have been less stressful had it not been for the times we are currently living through because at least then the opportunity was ample, but now here we are. Our new reality. He's trying to find us a way to stay afloat, and I'm trying to take care of our newborn while contemplating my route to helping us financially. And to be honest, I'm still not sure which way I am to go.

The Finances
from the perspective of Darwin Durr

Throughout this book, you may have seen that I've mentioned things that I consider as accomplishments. Accomplishments that once read, one would think that these acts have birthed a lot of money due to their contextual nature. Well, they haven't. The reader must understand that creating a product doesn't mean that it will materialize into a self-sustaining source of living. Thus far, all that I have managed to accomplish has not gotten Sarah and I to the point where we could single-handedly live off the success of that particular product. Granted, two of the projects haven't even become available to the market yet, so we don't know the potentiality of the ROI. The two are: this book and the mobile video game available worldwide on iOS and Android. Both are due to be released late May of this year.

Now, my first two books sold horribly. That was due to the lack of funds for one of the most essential aspects of creating a product: advertising. Not only that, it was due to my own personal fears of the controversial content that was within them. That caused me to not be as adamant in pushing them to be successful. However, when I say pushing them to be "successful", I'm speaking successful from a societal point of view – because in my eyes they are successes and plaques on the wall of my life.

Now, the clothing company is a different story. Sarah and I saved up some money and dropped an estimated $12,000 of that savings trying to get this thing off the ground. A lot of that $12,000 was a waste due to business ignorance. One of the biggest blunders and losses that we just figured out recently, is being tricked and deceived by a company in China. Seems like our luck with China is not so good now that I think of it. However, I was determined to be a highly successful young, African-American male who came from the lower echelons of life, to a self-made success. I'm still determined to reach that outcome, by the way.

Learning that products are made cheaper in China, I started searching and searching for a Chinese company that could design a sneaker for me. You see, the African-American community spends billions of dollars per year on sneakers alone. Therefore, I saw this as a way of entering a thriving market and that if I pulled this off, business would be amazing! So, I found a company located in China (I won't state their name), hired them, engaged in talks with them for about 45 days, and they produced for me what I believed to be a fantastic sneaker. Throughout this entire process, a representative from that company would periodically send me images of them manufacturing the shoe piece by piece. They sent images of just the sole of the shoe, followed by images of the tongue being designed, etc. I received emails saying that they were waiting for this piece and that piece. So, I was really under the impression that this shoe was being crafted from scratch (which I do think they actually built it from scratch) just for my company. They put my logo on the shoe and they even designed the boxes with my logo.

This was the highlight of my life. All I kept thinking was that my deceased godbrother, Aaron, would be extremely proud of this move. Aaron was a true sneaker head. He loved shoes. After the shoes had been fully manufactured, they were shipped to us in gigantic boxes. I felt like a boss for once! My wife received the delivery. She sent me a picture of the boxes via text while I was at work and said, "Look at your dream!"

Just when I thought that I was making the right moves in life, we later (recently) found out that we were deceived by this Chinese company that we hired to make the sneaker. This company, till this day I'm guessing, is [allegedly] engaged in intellectual property theft and the shoe that they crafted for us was actually a patent design (Patent design is being used in a speculative tense because we didn't actual look up the patent. We just assumed that the design of this sneaker had a patent because the U.S. company that we found to have an exact match to our shoe is a major company) by another U.S. famous and major company. So, we suddenly stopped selling that product and it has led to a major loss.

How did we figure this out? Well, someone on social media commented under one of our ads with a link that said, "Are those sneakers the same as these?" So, I clicked on the link and god-damn-it my heart dropped! At first, I thought it wasn't real. However, after going to the actual website of the company and seeing the exact replica of the sneaker that we had, and also doing a little further research, I was able to validate that the guy was correct. Holy shit, I thought. We stopped selling the sneaker and writing this is my first time actually telling the public about this disaster.

With all of my attempts to make something out of myself, something beyond normality, I still found myself needing a regular job. So, working as a server/somewhat bartender was my foundational source of income. However, in March 2020 that all changed. Due to COVID-19, I was laid off. Before I cut my days down to focus more on my small clothing company, I was bringing home about $1,200 a week. Once I cut my days down drastically, I was only bringing home about $700 a week. At the same time that I cut my days down drastically, my wife quit her salary job at an advertising agency and started driving for Lyft. The plan was to build our own prosperous business. "We're young and healthy, so what the hell do we have to lose?" we thought. First, it was a food truck idea. We had the money to buy a used truck and slowly refurbish it, but Washington, DC's regulations are so stringent that we decided to attempt something else. Besides, neither one of us is a chef! I'm just creative. I came up with a menu that had some unbelievably delicious dishes on them and they actually tasted great. I'll just tell you two of the items because we may later revamp this idea, so I don't want to give away everything. Two examples are: Crab Muffins and Strawberry Chicken!

Next, it was a laundromat idea. We actually contacted a realtor that was an agent for acquisition businesses and he gave us an address and info of a small laundromat for sale in Maryland. Sarah and I went to check it out and we fell in love with the idea of pursuing this. We had a BOMB business plan written for this place. It was unbelievably innovative and futuristic! We hired a firm for $2,000 (big mistake), to help us get additional funding to meet the asking down payment of the owner. This firm initially told us that this process would take two weeks. It ended up being two months! So, we canceled the contract with them because the laundromat had been sold. We couldn't get our money back because of the fine print on the contract (hey, you live and you learn). So, the end result materialized into a clothing company. Sarah and I operated in that capacity for about a year. Then came the triple big bang: COVID-19, loss of job, and a newborn child. ALL AT ONCE!

Our clothing business stopped functioning because like the sneakers, 80% of our clothing products are designed in China. However, the clothing is actually our own designs. So, there aren't any intellectual property theft issues with that. Anyway, the company that we dealt with shut down their production, so we had to pause our website. To be honest, the business wasn't doing that good anyway. Our cost was extremely higher than our profits. We were spending way more money on advertisement per month than we were profiting in sales.

Now, how does this all fit into the book theme of 1 house, 2 minds, the psychological effects of COVID-19? About two months into our one-year process of trying to build our own business, Sarah's interest started to fade. Her input became less and less. It got so bad that I just started taking the lead and eventually the clothing business felt like mine's alone. This angered me in the beginning because together we decided to make this tremendous sacrifice of working our regular jobs less and focusing a lot more on our own business. If I knew that she was going to give up on me (business-wise), the sacrifice could've been executed much differently and it could have been a lot less extreme, rather than her quitting her salary job and me cutting my days down at my regular job.

This became the sentiment of our household. I woke up every day as a relentless dreamer, and she woke up and just existed. I was spending every spare dollar, outside of our bill money, trying to build a business engine. I was reinvesting all of our profits as well, which essentially left us broke all the time. I was determined to merge fashion and technology. I started designing our clothes with QR-Codes that led to our website, as a fashionable marker on the attire. It was neat. If someone were to ask the wearer where he or she got their clothing item from, they could say, "Scan here!" I came up with this idea of designing winter coats that came with electronic tablets. I placed a tablet in the inner pocket of each coat that was sold. Even though it was two different products, I psychologically made them appear as one by the way I marketed them.

Everything we sold I wanted to have a technological component to it. I had cartoon commercials created for us. I hired fashion models to model our clothing. I designed and created our own magazine. I started a YouTube channel for the business with a segment called, Table Presentations, where I would show off our products. I started learning how to sew. I wrote two beautiful theme songs for our business and hired two different singers to sing the lyrics. I paid them as well as paid for the studio time. On one of the songs, not only did I write the lyrics, I also played the piano instrumentation. I started a blog for our website. I created this saying: A Bombardment of Intrigue. Essentially, what that meant was to never give the public the chance to perceive you as a failure. Flood their eyes with a shit-ton of content!

My drive was impeccable, but there just wasn't enough money to take it to the extremes in which I wanted. I wanted to go global. My targeted goal was to create some sort of clothing product that could project holograms. That was just one of my hopes. However, throughout this entire process, the journey became lonelier and lonelier.

Things started really getting intense during Sarah's 7th month of pregnancy which was in December of 2019. Even though our business had an excellent December. Sarah started working her job a lot less due to the baby. The following month, January 2020, she stopped working altogether. Little did we both know, a virus was approaching during the same time. So, money was already beginning to get extremely tight because the entire onus of the house responsibilities was falling on me and I secretly felt like I couldn't handle it.

Bang… Zehn Issa Durr was born in February of 2020! Bang… COVID-19 became a pandemic and I lost my job in March of 2020 due its arrival! Bang… All hell broke loose! "What the hell do I do now?" I thought! My clarity of thought is stuck within thick mud. The unemployment system is archaic and worthless, and Congress is so ideologically partisan and divided that assistance for the American people may take forever! It's moments like this where darkness begins to shine brighter than the light. Your thoughts convene a meeting in your head, and you begin debates about dignity versus malevolence. "Do I approach this situation in a dignified manner, or do I join the illuminating darkness?" Reliance on our elected leaders are so frail, that you begin inching closer and closer to that radiating dimness. You become broken.

On the day my job told me not to come in, I made some moves to sure up enough funds to get us through at least a month, barely. But, the pressure of racing a debt clock is heavy. At that same time, I was trying to apply for unemployment. It took me literally three weeks just to get through to a representative to get my claim processed. Once processed, the very nice lady on the phone said that my claim may take up to 21 days to be verified and processed further. WHAT! So, I waited three weeks to get through. Now, I have to wait an additional 21 days to even receive a dollar from the same system that is forcing me to stay home and not be able to make my own dollar?! LIVID!

A depressing cloud orbits your head when a system that is put in place to help and assist is derelict – especially when it never seems to malfunction when it's taking your taxes. We hear our whole American life that this is the greatest country in the world, but the validity of that statement is really on trial right now. How in the hell can any government system, whether it's state, local, or federal, not be functioning on updated apparatuses that fit these modern times of technical velocity?

When you begin to watch a full fridge of food become a few packs of noodles in your cabinet, it's like watching a robbery take place and there's nothing that you can do about it. There's no police to call, there's no judge to rule. The robbery is at liberty to proceed.

Dignity versus malevolence. I chose a sacrificial dignity. Instead of allowing the darkness to lure me in, I instead figured that I'll put my talents to use and try to "artist" my way out of this situation. What other options are there? Nothing's open and no one's hiring. So, I borrowed money from my mother. Which pained me to do so because of her disbelief in dismantling normality. However, instead of stashing that money, I made the sacrifice of writing and publishing two books and creating a mobile video game and using the residuals to advertise all three products. I was once told by a therapist that I had a gambling gene embedded in me. I guess it's true.

I figured, I have to try something. This is not to shame my wife, but she just doesn't seem interested in the preservation of our security and wellbeing. If she does, she doesn't show it. Her pace of conceptualizing the crisis that we're in is somewhat that of a tortoise. I mentioned in another chapter (The Newborn) of how within the last 60 days, I've been trying all I can to bring an extra dollar into the house – without doing anything criminal. You see, criminality has an art to it. The art is, "instant reward." Though that instant reward usually results in further destruction, the lure lives within the moment, not the future.

I often wonder what kind of a team my wife and I would be if she had the same drive as me. With her college degree and my relentless drive and creative mind, I always felt like we could potentially do much better in life. But when it's just me, and only me, chasing dreams and hunting opportunities, it makes it harder because being attached to someone that isn't moving is like being anchored. With our finances at nearly zero, I really wish that she had a blackboard full of ideas that we could also chase. This makes it harder.

I'll end by saying: "Dear God, if You're up there, not just Sarah and I, but the world in its entirety could really use a blessing. This creation, earth, and man is too beautiful to allow destabilization to ugly its future. I'm not asking for a handout; I'm asking for a hand. I'm asking that You reach downwards of the billows, careful of the passing pigeons, and grab the hand of this peasant and pull me from my knees. Clear my eyes of the mud; clean my ears of the cacophonies of despair. Make me whole again. Allow me to be that hero that Sarah, Zehn, and Jaccai need. Make me immune to the kryptonite. Show this wolf how to hunt. Amen.

Finding an Enemy
from the perspective of Sarah Durr

Ever seen the movie *Castaway*? Yeah, well, if I was on lockdown in my home by myself for months I'm pretty sure I'd find *something* to pick a fight with, too. It's human nature. Even while being in solitude, we find ourselves getting irritable, antsy, agitated. Adding another person into the equation just makes the frustration easier to justify when it's let out. Quite frankly, it doesn't take as much to get tired of being up under or around the same individual(s) when it seems like nothing new is occurring in your surroundings. No spark, no excitement… just the same old thing day after day, after day. Next thing you know, an argument arises over who had the remote last before it went missing. Pure nonsense somehow becomes justifiably-enough to create "something out of nothing." An instance such as the effects of the pandemic are enough to cause much disruption in one's household, and I'm not just referring to the economic aspect of it all. Many people either implicitly or deliberately start to look for someone to blame, or to take their frustrations out on. In others words, we can probably all admit to have been: Finding an Enemy.

Whether it was your governor whose newly-sanctioned restrictions you opposed, or the media pundit who profusely defended it on the news that pissed you off—you likely let that steam off somewhere… Or, on someone. (Did you just realize how many times you subliminally did that in the past few months?) Redirecting anger is a real thing, and something that I'm willing to bet occurred in quarantined-homes all across the country throughout the duration of this pandemic thus far.

When the coronavirus first reached the brinks of a pandemic issue, I recall a phone call I had with one of my cousins who lives overseas in the Netherlands. We started to converse about the new reality most of the world's population was facing and she made a comment that I had originally taken as a joke. She said, "Think about how many divorces will come out of this when it's over." And as I said, I thought she was joking, so I laughed it off and suggested another, "Or, how many babies." (I wasn't joking.) But, getting back to her suggestion, I started to realize the truth in what she said as the weeks continued to go on.

Not only on the news, but even in my own home, the psychological effects of this pandemic were starting to take a toll on our psyches. Levels of cortisol, the stress hormone, were rising by the day to the point that I could not foresee a decline in sight. It seemed like anything could start a problem between us. We could literally go from having a somewhat decent day to all of the sudden stalking the local city official updates trying to decipher, "How much longer of this sh*t?!" Too many times to count, my husband abruptly left the house full of frustration from an argument; and, my annoyance continued to grow as I had no choice but to stay in the house with our newborn daughter.

There was always something to unearth controversy over. Even our views on the pandemic, itself, started to cause confrontation. "Should people be staying home?" "When is it really safe for businesses to start to reopen?" "Is this whole thing a conspiracy?" So many questions with, ultimately, just a bunch of subjective opinions for answers. No one could bring us comfort with their stats, or predictions, or so-called words of hope. Not Dr. Anthony Fauci, not the president, not the media, and certainly not the irritating housemates we're all locked down with!

Even when we started to hear about the peak beginning to reach a decline countrywide, the news still hits us with an update of "3 more months of restrictions" in some parts of the country. And we can't forget talks about another resurgence anticipated to reoccur by the fall. Hmm… So, if you're doing the math, what they're actually telling those of us who are paying attention is: 3 more months + resurgence in the fall = We aren't reopening anytime soon.

We observed tens of thousands of Americans yearning for work, for their children to return back to school, to get a haircut, etc. as they protested in the streets of Michigan and California, amongst other places. Then, we watched as health care workers also counter-protested, urging more Americans to attempt to slow the spread by making the conscious effort to stay home instead. Like almost everything else in the States, people were starting to make it all out to be a red versus blue issue, even though the virus seemed to be operating as a color-blind agent.

I'm so curious to find out how many psychologists are currently studying the emotional toll that is taking effect on citizens' psyches and what they end up concluding from their findings. It has to be astronomical levels of anxiety across the board. There are so many factors that would contribute to an increase in depression and anxiety. The impact of losing loved ones, to start. Grandparents, parents, friends, co-workers. Some folks left their places of employment just weeks ago and will return with less staff when those businesses reopen. The loss of employment for many, or even worse, those losing their own businesses. Imagine working to create your own business, your baby essentially, for years (maybe decades) and have that totally upended in a matter of weeks with nothing you can do to prevent it. And, of course, the unknown nature of all of this. The best we can do is predict how long this may go on for and hope like hell things will get better instead of worse from here, but the fact of the matter is we just don't know either of those outcomes.

The psychological effects that this pandemic has created were unimaginable just earlier this year. The economy was booming, jobs were plentiful, and I, for one, absolutely took that for granted in comparison to how quickly things have fallen flat. When I made the decision to stay at home with Zehn after she was born, I still had in the back of my mind the notion that I could always go get a job if our new dynamic as a one-income household wasn't a plausible fit. Whether it was working from home, or outside the home part-time or full-time, I never considered something like this [pandemic] would occur and limit the ability for me to even have that option. Now, it seems as though women and men who never imagined being stay-at-home parents, have experienced becoming just that within this short period. The abrupt nature of this invisible beast and its effects has left us all reminded that God laughs when He hears us speak of our plans.

Even our children are feeling the psychological effects of it. At first, for the life of me I could not understand why my step-son, who has always been an honor-roll student, was showing a lack of motivation to complete his schooling from home. In my mind, it was the easier option between actually attending 5 eight-hour school days versus a few hours of Zoom teleconferences a week from home! I've experienced working from home in the past and I absolutely preferred it to going into my then-workplace. I figured the same would be true for kids that are now schooling from home. Shorter days, later classes, less classes. Wearing pajama bottoms instead of the usually-required uniform. It sounded like a kid's dream turned into reality! But, I was completely wrong. He hated the new dynamic. He even said he'd prefer to go back to his usual school schedule as opposed to tuning into those Zoom sessions and doing work out of thick binders that seemed to never end. Frustration has been sprouting from his end, as well, and to no fault of his own. We've all found ourselves just trying to make the best out of a situation no one predicted would now be our reality.

So, as you could imagine the tension is getting thicker by the day in our home. Simple gestures now say so much in such little noise. The slam of a binder, pulling out of a chair, locking of the front door. All of which have become reasons to suspect attitude coming from that direction. Inevitably, being cooped up in a small, one-bedroom apartment with nothing but time, anxiety, a teenager and a demanding baby, calls for just a matter of time before things start to get contentious. Not that I had been anticipating it, but… I mean, come on. As the calendar pages kept flipping, Darwin was turning into a ticking. time. bomb. Literally. The most minute instances (to me, anyways) triggered this guy into a whirlwind of a frenzy that always lead back to the same rant ending in: "…and don't you realize how serious this situation could potentially get for us???!?"

Now, I will admit—naturally, my demeanor is very much like that of a hippie. Calm, cool and collected, if you will. I'm an "out-of-sight, out-of-mind" type of person, so the constant lingering of any one thought is not a likely culprit in my life. And it may just be to my detriment one day, but then again, it may be what's saving my sanctity. Darwin and I differ in this way. It's not likely that you'll catch me making a widely-dramatized scene about much, but I can't exactly say the same for my dear husband. Have you ever seen the movie *2012*? My husband is pretty much like that one character Woody Harrelson played that was kind of a nut job, but is right about what he's flailing on about, so it's like you shouldn't *totally* tune him out when he goes into rant mode… but then again, does he *really* have to be so theatrical to get his point across? But again, we differ. I often thought it was these kinds of differences between us that made us work well with one another, picking up where the other lacks; but, during this coronavirus pandemic, it just seemed to have driven us even further apart.

A vast difference in communication styles also intensifies debates occurring these days. My husband is very animated and extremely pronounced in how he chooses to express himself. It took me a long time to accept that it's just the way he is, but it can really rub a person the wrong way if they aren't into such animation. Seemed to me like he was always just "doing too much." However, I can admit that my communication isn't much better. It's actually often a lack thereof, so I realize that contributes in large part to our strife, as well. Blame it on my cultural upbringing. We have a tendency to refrain from diving into taboo subjects, subjects that are far from secret in a lot of the households my American peers grew up in. I was always amazed by that difference coming from my Eritrean household. That distinction has influenced my expressive side in a way that hinders me from truly being at ease with vulnerability. At times, I feel like a mute. Thoughts running through my mind from one end to the other through the labyrinth of brain cells, yet my lips won't part to utter them. I've come to realize a lot of this behavior stems from a fear of saying the wrong thing, and being criticized for it. Many times, the exact thoughts that I'm pondering make perfect sense in my mind, but then they are phrased entirely wrong. The inability to effectively communicate with your partner will likely already result in continuous dispute, but under the confines of the coronavirus lockdown, tensions are heightened even further.

Let me paint you a scenario of what any given day can turn into with us:

Irritant – When I *just* finally get the baby to sleep and here comes my husband, moseying back into our tiny apartment (from wherever he got to run off to in order to clear his mind) and he comes in making noise. Well, so much for that nap – baby is now up. Great! (Sense the sarcasm. That also triggers a lot of our "attitudes gone bad." Not to mention I tend to speak with my face a lot, or so I'm told. I may not be very expressive verbally, but these facials expressions sure are.) Now, I have an attitude—if I didn't already! Because while he was out letting off some steam, I was still locked down brewing up some more in here. So, whatever relief he likely experienced outside of this tension-filled home, he's now right back in the thick of it with the rest of us who've just been basking in it since he left.

cues the start of new argument

Have you ever realized how much tension can fill up the air the smaller a space becomes? It's like dealing with humidity or heat. You box it in, and it feels like it's smothering you. That's what our one-bedroom sometimes feels like. And, keep in mind it's not like we can just freely go here or there every time we get into a dispute because, oh yeah, nothing is open! Now think about how many scenarios, like such, have occurred over the past few months that we've been cooped up in this house together. Yeah, I couldn't count them either.

And the tension is coming from every which way, it seems like. My step-son, Jac, is frustrated with schooling from home. My husband, Darwin, is tired of telling him to get it together. Our daughter, Zehn, is simply playing her role as a sporadically-crying baby which then causes disruption in Darwin's attempts to concentrate on his thoughts, so that reflects in irritability from him. I'm feeling like I'm walking on eggshells around him cause when he gets like this it's only a matter of time before another scenario such as the previously given one becomes of itself once again. Starting trivial and extending to another hours-long rant ending in: "…and don't you realize how serious this situation could potentially get for us???!?"

There's a ripple effect that takes place and seems never-ending. (Since all of these days just seem to clash into one, big "yesterday.") I sometimes wonder if my husband appears so anxious because of how fast he's trying to move or if he's moving at that speed to keep up with his anxiety. Another way we differ. We don't move at the same speed. I do things at my own pace and for a reason — mainly for the peace of mind. (I told y'all I'm somewhat of a hippie.) With the many external factors we do not have control over in our lives, this is at least one matter I do have some aspect of control over: my anxiety. While anxiety is at an all-time high for many, topping it off with added pressure coming from your own household just feels like there isn't any escaping the stress. So, where would one be to go from there? But again, it's human nature. We are all looking for someone [or something] to take our frustrations out on. Even if that something turns out to just be Wilson.

Finding an Enemy
from the perspective of Darwin Durr

There are so many tiny things that aggregate together into an annoying attribute of your spouse that is usually overlooked, or that is tolerable. However, they can quickly metastasize into an irritant that is unbearable when something like COVID-19 becomes the only thing walking outside – and all humans are forced to stay indoors.

Sometimes I feel like people fail to understand that the context of love and the context of work are one in itself. People get stuck, relishing in the honeymoon state of mind while becoming completely oblivious to that fact that relationships have tiers. It's almost impossible for a relationship to manifest the same freedoms of euphoria the further you go into it. Why? Because the further you go into it, the more responsibilities that you adopt and add to it – and responsibilities bear a friction-like energy because most responsibilities come with a binary option of success or failure based on the amount of input by those in the relationship. That creates a strain on the relationship. Therefore, that's why there are tiers. The tiers are designed to keep a balance. First, it's the honeymoon tier, but then there's the partnership tier. The partnership tier is where the honeymoon sparks are a tad bit less, but the reduction is refilled by the worth of the responsibilities that you as partners have adopted. Responsibilities like children, etc.

On this understanding alone, I think that this is where Sarah and I start to veer. I think she still yearns for that honeymoon tier, but moments like now, with the COVID-19 destroying our livelihood, we need our partnership to take precedence versus dwelling in a honeymoon state of mind.

Sarah and I already had our differences pre-COVID-19. We are quite different ideologically. However, different ideological positions are tolerable, until muddy waters come about and the solutions for getting out of them require a collaborative consensus, in other words, a partnership. The lockdown has caused our differences to mutate into a new strand of problems. It has raised questions about our connectivity during tough times and the strength of our ability to be resilient as a union.

One house, two different minds. I view this lockdown as a war on the psyche, puncture wounds to our livelihood, and a forced stagnation resulting in an unforeseeable future. What I witness from Sarah's out loud reaction to this crisis is more nonchalant – at least that's the reactive projection that I get from her. This divides us on a daily basis as of late. I'm waking up every morning with a ferocious and relentless drive to preserve our balance, and she awakens seeming to ignore the tick tocks of the clock and showing no signs of concern that the day of reckoning may be approaching our doorstep pretty soon. Money is hemorrhaging, bills are rolling around, groceries are depleting, unemployment insurance is taking about a month to kick in, and me getting my job back doesn't look promising.

I'm honestly perplexed as of how to resolve these disparities. On one hand, I feel like I should be solely adopting every burden that passes through our home, no matter how stringent. On the other hand, I admit that I hide the fact that my mental infrastructure and financial capability to do so are in dire need of a partnership, for I am unable to do it alone. To say this aloud makes me feel less of a man. I try to paint this picture like I can handle everything alone, but that is far from the truth. This is largely due to the competitive nature of a man and the insecurities that comes with that. Maybe it's my insecurities that are blockading me from a verbal admittance to my wife that I desperately need her to step up and be a more active partner for the betterment of our home.

My insecurities are scornful. I believe every struggling man with a beautiful wife houses a clandestine thought of his wife leaving him for someone in a much better position. Whether it's true or not, the thought sits in your head every moment that you fail to build a stable foundation for your household, and it adds pressure the further you get closer to failure.

However, what concerns me, despite my "I can handle everything" sentiment, is my wife's inability to know when to intercept with contributing preventative measures. Even though I say that I can handle everything, she clearly sees me hovering just slightly above complete failure. That's like a swimming pool lifeguard watching someone drowning and lets them drown because prior to going into the pool the person said that they could swim. This compromises my trust in her judgment and her ability to have strategic foresight. I always say this to her, "You know… some people can't talk. So, you gotta learn to read people." There's a deep message within that saying, especially for married couples. You should know your spouse like the back of your hand. When they're moping, sobbing, smiling, dreadful, gleeful, stressed, holding back, etc., you should know the mechanisms as of how to interject yourself in the proper manner to contribute to any one of those states of mind that they're displaying, as a partner. So, because my wife more than often fails at reading me, it makes me feel like a loner on every journey that I embark on – and I embark on a lot.

Coming from the ghettos of Washington, DC, born during the era of crack cocaine and when this city was classified as the murder capital of the country, I've never seen nor met anyone who aspires to, "in a legit manner", climb as much as me. When I say climb, I mean deviating from the structural norms of the status quo. Veering from the life routes that are preordained by a societal narrative of expectations. For example, my ears get pulverized by voices that say college is the only way. Yet, my innate passions to be productive exceed most college students' productivity levels. Without a degree or a lecture from a professor, I've written and published 4 books total (2 within the last 60 days), written/recorded over one-thousand literature rich songs, started a small clothing business, created my own mobile video game available worldwide for iOS and Android devices, defeated severe alcoholism without any licensed/professional help whatsoever, reprogrammed my entire mindset, learned about business, became steep within politics, and married a beautiful, college-educated woman from a middleclass household, something I never had the luxury of having. So, my journey has been quite a ride.

Yet, those that I would have imagined being the proudest of my deviations from what my destitute environment paints as normalcy, my mother and my wife – see no magic within my phenomenal accomplishments. There's no one else in my family that consistently chases a success based on talent and innate passions. It's all a race to the same systems. An encapsulation within collectivized desires like working for the government or finding a blue-collar job that just gets you by. Nothing captures my mother's validation besides a government job. If I don't have a government job, then all else is buffoonery. But I understand that archaic mindset very well. That mindset of settling with the surface and having no interest in defying gravity. So, my mom doesn't surprise me too much. However, my wife… Well, that's a different story. My wife understands fully what the future requires. My wife understands that technology and innovation are the keys to modern success. She understands, through voices like Mark Cuban and Dave Ramsey, that hard work and a relentless pursuit is how you finance your calendars to come. So, when she sees her husband bussing his butt and mass-producing things/ideas and trying his hardest to explore different routes to success, I would expect that she would be my biggest cheerleader and my most reliable partner. But she is really finding it hard to execute that "partner" aspect. She's still on the honeymoon tier.

Being on two different tiers, Sarah on the honeymoon tier, me on the partnership tier, is what causes the confliction in our household. COVID-19 is a severe blow to our home and I'm approaching it with seriousness and in dire need of my wife to enter the partnership tier so that we can fight this thing together. This disparity makes me appear angry around the house, but it's not necessarily anger. It's a radiation of mass focus because these times are quite familiar to me because of my upbringing and I'm fully cognizant of the fact that it's going to take a warrior spirit to prevail. However, I believe this irritates Sarah because my persona probably comes off more so "drill sergeant" than "charismatic". I'm sorry, but WE'RE IN A PANDEMIC!

I think the difference between us when it comes to approaching situations that are severe, like the COVID-19, is the difference in our upbringings. When I get Sarah irritated by what she may deem as having a "drill sergeant" persona, I think she fails to analyze the difference between our environmental and experiential upbringing. There's a vast difference psychologically between her middleclass upbringing and my impoverished upbringing. The parental security system built around her upbringing heavily mitigated her exposure to crisis. Therefore, when she sees the predicament that COVID-19 has placed us in, it's almost as if she believes that it'll magically disperse on its own, and not by the hard attempts by "us" to mitigate its damage as much as possible. I was exposed to the perilous sides of life growing up. My streetlights were Satan's eyes. The only way to make it out of those conditions was to ferociously fight a stagnated system designed to keep us entrapped within it. You had no choice but to familiarize yourself with chaos and disaster.

So, one can see why my approach to life bears a more serious approach. During this COVID-19 pandemic, I'm literally fixated on the data associated with it. I'm studying it like a student writing a thesis paper. I'm consistently reading about it. I don't allow my television to change from the news. Cable news plays in my house 24/7. I'm checking our Mayor's comments and strategies daily. I'm reading everyday about new cases, the areas that are showing increases and decreases, new symptoms, states that are reopening slowly, states that are not, etc. I'm fixated on reality. I'm staying informed because I'm mapping out strategies while at the same time keeping up with the time limit of an approaching household disaster. This is not the same for Sarah. It's like she's in another world. If I ask her when the "stay-at-home" order is due to expire in our city, she wouldn't know. This drives me nuts! Why? Because this knowledge is pertinent to our survival. How can one be faced with an approaching disaster and not be studying its every move?

This explains the difference in our temperament. I see the axioms of life; she has a more fantasized vernacular. Her upbringing has left her dormant in a secure mindset where psychologically she feels shielded from the perils of life. The devil isn't familiar to her. Me, I know the guy pretty well. The way he operates and all.

This "1 house, 2 minds" scenario only works when liberty is afforded to us. Not when we're forcefully bounded to the four walls of an apartment. Liberties allow us to find other outlets. Outlets like going to work, going to the movies, road trips, going outside, going to a restaurant, visiting family, hanging out with friends, etc. Liberties that have the power of brief distractions from the ills of life. Liberties that can prevent from having to find an enemy in each other, because instead, we would find fun, joy, and peace. COVID-19 has stolen our freedom.

COLLABORATIVE SOLUTIONS

This chapter is a newly-created, innovative way, created by us, to allow the reader to become even more engaged with the authors and the messages being conveyed. Instead of writing this chapter out, we digitized it into a video of us actually discussing aloud our issues at hand.

SCAN the QR-CODE below with your smartphone camera and the link to the video will appear!

Click the link that appears on your phone and you will be directed to our 4th chapter: "Collaborative Solutions."

We hope you enjoy!

*Please check out Darwin's other new book, *Satan's Old Piano.*
Also available on Amazon only!
It is full of eroticism, action, and adventure!

*Also, please download our new mobile video game,
Mr. President, I Found The Cure.
The game is based on surviving the coronavirus.
Action-packed and fun to play!
Available worldwide on iOS and Android.

If for any reason, this video becomes no longer available via YouTube, email us at darwintheauthor@gmail.com for access to view Chapter 4, "Collaborative Solutions."

You can find our clothing brand at www.uththebrand.com

We appreciate all your support. Stay strong.